I0390437

Course on Certified Business Analysis Professional (CBAP®)

This course is fully aligned with BABOK® Version 2.0 of IIBA® and extensively covers topics that are essential for today's business analysts. The course unravels the business analysis concepts and techniques with practical examples that can be readily applied in your day-to-day work.

Course Benefits: The participants will gain a sound understanding in conducting and managing business analysis projects and also prepare themselves for the Certified Business Analysis Professional (CBAP®)* certification. [CBAP® is a registered trademark of International Institute of Business Analysis (IIBA®), Canada].

For more details, please visit www.bacourse.com

1. What is Business Analysis?

Business analysis is the combined application of domain expertise, business analysis tools & techniques and soft skills to coordinate among the stakeholders to analyse the organizations structure, policies and operations to come up with a solution to solve the organizations need or problems or opportunity.

In business analysis the business analyst is helping the organization to satisfy a business need or to solve a business problem or to utilize an opportunity.

2. Who is a Business Analyst?

Business Analyst is the person who recommends solution to the organization to help the organization to satisfy a need, to solve a problem and to utilise an opportunity.

3. Why Business Analysis?

Business Analysis is carried out for the following reasons:

a) Cross Functional Expertise:

In a functional hierarchy people are used to get expertise only in that particular department such as HR, Sales, Accounting, Marketing, Operations etc. And because of their long association and experience in the same department their knowledge is very much limited only to that department and they could not appreciate the roles and contribution in other departments.

In such a vacuum, business analysis and business analyst are becoming a required force in understanding all the departments and fill this vacuum.

b) Project Research:

Organizations are dynamic in nature. They have primarily two major responsibilities. One is their day-to-day operations and the other is planning for the future. Business Analysts' important contribution is primarily under this future contribution. Most of the project an organization undertakes is to implement or to bring in new capabilities that these organizations never had in the past.

In such circumstances it becomes very important that someone should dedicate and focus in learning about their new area and helps the organization and its members to understand the new capabilities.

c) Estimate Resources:

In any new projects rather than just jumping into the project it is better to thoroughly understand the resources required to successfully carryout and operate the project. Typically the various resources required for the project are Man, Machine, Material, Money and Capabilities. Business Analysis helps us to understand, what all are the solution requirements that a project should satisfy and based on that, all the resources required could be easily estimated. So, when a business analysis is carried out, it is a detailed project report or a business plan that helps the organization to better estimate the resources and commit the resources.

d) To create a shade understanding:

People in an organization working vertical silos for a long period of time could not easily understand about other departments and their functioning. In this scenario they cannot easily implement a project that is spreading across several departments in an organization. Because of this we need business analysis and business analyst to create a unified understanding or shade understanding among the stakeholders of the project working in various departments. Because of the business analyst expertise working in cross functional teams seeing the bigger picture of the project, he or she is always focussed on the organizational requirement rather than having a parochial view.

e) Fine-tune the Requirements:

Because of business analysts' experience in business analysis tasks and techniques he or she can easily pull out the requirements from the stakeholders and unify and validate those requirements. Thus guarantees capturing right requirements that will certainly add value to the organization.

f) To achieve high success rate in Project Implementation:

A Business Analyst is a person who has expert level skills in Business Analysis and Sound Knowledge in the industry. With such a combination he will be able to gather the right requirements and also verify them whether it is implementable and also assess them whether it will meet the solution requirements. This exercise enhances the success rate of project implementation. In other words, Business Analyst helps the organization to conceive design and operate a project on a piece of paper.

4. What is a Domain?

Domain is the area in which the business analysis project is going to be carried out. Any business analyst before embarking on a business analysis project should define the domain. This will help the Business Analyst to have a boundary in which he or she will operate. Domain helps the business analyst to focus and study only those relevant processes and system that will be affected and will affect the business analysis project. In summary domain helps the business analyst to optimize his working by setting a boundary.

5. What is Domain Expertise?

In casual discussions the terms 'domain' and 'domain expertise' are interchangeably used but they have significantly different meanings in business analysis. Domain is the area undergoing the business analysis. On the other hand domain expertise is the vertical in which the business analyst is working. The examples of domain expertise are Health care, Hospitality, Insurance, Banking, Finance, Engineering, Construction, IT etc.

6. What is a Solution?

Solution is the prescription to the problem or a need or an opportunity. The ultimate deliverable from a business analyst is the solution. Solution is the recommended system, procedure and capabilities from the business analyst that will help the organization to reach its goals and objectives.

7. What is a Task?

A Task is a group of business analysis activities that are carried out to move forward in a business analysis project. BABOK version 2 of IIBA, Canada recommends 32 tasks that are grouped under 6 knowledge areas. By carrying out the tasks in a planned and iterative manner, the business analyst wades through an uncharted see to find out the solution and recommends it to the organization. Task is a business analysis step that helps the business analyst to march forward towards his unknown solution.

8. What is Elicitation?

Elicitation is the process of pulling out the requirements from the stakeholder. In other words, elicitation is drawing out the requirements from the mouth of stakeholders. It is the responsibility of the business analyst to gather all the requirements. Business analyst should be skilful in gathering the requirements using the various BA tools and techniques. Only BA will be blamed for a poor requirement and nobody else in an organization. There is a complete knowledge area dedicated for elicitation in BABOK of IIBA, Canada. The four tasks included under elicitation are

   a. Prepare for elicitation
   b. Conduct elicitation activity
   c. Document Elicitation Results
   d. Confirm Elicitation Results

9. What are Organizational Process Assets?

The outcomes of various business analysis and process improvement efforts are stored in a repository within an organization for future use. This is to avoid doing the same work in a future date. Moreover before embarking on a business analysis project, the business analyst must go through the organizational process assets to get a good understanding of what had happened in the past in his or her area of proposed research. Today organizations rely on the IT enabled tools such as Enterprise Content Management for storing organizational process assets. But in other cases, they use a physical library to index and store the business analysis and process improvement documents.

10. What is Process Improvement?

Process improvement is understanding the gaps in the current process and taking it to the next improved level. There are various schools of thinking in process improvement such as Lean, Six Sigma, Total Quality Management, Re-engineering etc.

11. Explain Lean?

The core idea is to maximize customer value while minimizing waste. Simply, lean means creating more value for customers with fewer resources. A lean organization understands customer value and focuses its key processes to continuously increase it. The ultimate goal is to provide perfect value to the customer through a perfect value creation process that has zero waste.

To accomplish this, lean thinking changes the focus of management from optimizing separate technologies, assets, and vertical departments to optimizing the flow of products and services through entire value streams that flow horizontally across technologies, assets, and departments to customers.

Eliminating waste along entire value streams, instead of at isolated points, creates processes that need less human effort, less space, less capital, and less time to make products and services at far less costs and with much fewer defects, compared with traditional business systems. Companies are able to respond to changing customer desires with high variety, high quality, low cost, and with very fast throughput times. Also, information management becomes much simpler and more accurate.

The espoused goals of lean manufacturing systems differ between various authors. While some maintain an internal focus, e.g. to increase profit for the organization, others claim that improvements should be done for the sake of the customer

Some commonly mentioned goals are:
- Improve quality
- Eliminate waste
- Reduce time
- Reduce total costs

The strategic elements of lean can be quite complex, and comprise multiple elements. Four different notions of lean identified are:
1. Lean as a fixed state or goal (being lean)
2. Lean as a continuous change process (becoming lean)
3. Lean as a set of tools or methods (doing lean/toolbox lean)
4. Lean as a philosophy (lean thinking)

12. Explain Six Sigma?

Six Sigma is a highly disciplined process that helps us focus on developing and delivering near-perfect products and services.

Why "Sigma"? The word is a statistical term that measures how far a given process deviates from perfection. The central idea behind Six Sigma is that if you can measure how many "defects" you have in a process, you can systematically figure out how to eliminate them and get as close to "zero defects" as possible.

Six Sigma has evolved over the last two decades and so has its definition. Six Sigma has literal, conceptual, and practical definitions.

Six Sigma at three different levels:
- As a metric
- As a methodology
- As a management system

Six Sigma as a Metric

The term "Sigma" is often used as a scale for levels of "goodness" or quality. Using this scale, "Six Sigma" equates to 3.4 defects per one million opportunities (DPMO). Therefore, Six Sigma started as a defect reduction effort in manufacturing and was then applied to other business processes for the same purpose.

Six Sigma as a Methodology

As Six Sigma has evolved, there has been less emphasis on the literal definition of 3.4 DPMO, or counting defects in products and processes. Six Sigma is a business improvement methodology that focuses an organization on:

- Understanding and managing customer requirements
- Aligning key business processes to achieve those requirements
- Utilizing rigorous data analysis to minimize variation in those processes
- Driving rapid and sustainable improvement to business processes

At the heart of the methodology is the DMAIC model for process improvement. DMAIC is commonly used by Six Sigma project teams and is an acronym for:

- Define opportunity
- Measure performance
- Analyse opportunity
- Improve performance
- Control performance

Six Sigma Management System

When practiced as a management system, Six Sigma is a high performance system for executing business strategy. Six Sigma is a top-down solution to help organizations:

- Align their business strategy to critical improvement efforts
- Mobilize teams to attack high impact projects
- Accelerate improved business results
- Govern efforts to ensure improvements are sustained

The Six Sigma Management System drives clarity around the business strategy and the metrics that most reflect success with that strategy. It provides the framework to prioritize resources for projects that will improve the metrics, and it leverages leaders who will manage the efforts for rapid, sustainable, and improved business results.

Quality management tools and methods used in Six Sigma

Within the individual phases of a DMAIC or DMADV project, Six Sigma utilizes many established quality-management tools that are also used outside Six Sigma. The following table shows an overview of the main methods used.

- 5 Whys
- Analysis of variance/General linear model/ANOVA Gauge R&R/Regression/Correlation/Scatter diagram/Chi-squared test of independence and fits
- Axiomatic design
- Business Process Mapping/Check sheet
- Cause & effects diagram (also known as fishbone or Ishikawa diagram)
- Control chart/Control plan (also known as a swim lane map)/Run charts Six Sigma 4
- Cost-benefit analysis
- CTQ tree
- Design of experiments/Stratification
- Histograms/Pareto analysis/Pareto chart
- Pick chart/Process capability/Rolled throughput yield
- Quality Function Deployment (QFD)
- Quantitative marketing research through use of Enterprise Feedback Management (EFM) systems
- Root cause analysis
- SIPOC analysis (Suppliers, Inputs, Process, Outputs, Customers)
- COPIS analysis (Customer centric version/perspective of SIPOC)
- Taguchi methods/Taguchi Loss Function
- Value stream mapping

13. Explain Total Quality Management (TQM)?

Total Quality Management (TQM) is a management approach that originated in the 1950s and has steadily become more popular since the early 1980s. Total quality is a description of the culture, attitude and organization of a company that strives to provide customers with products and services that satisfy their needs. The culture requires quality in all aspects of the company's operations, with processes being done right the first time and defects and waste eradicated from operations.

To be successful implementing TQM, an organization must concentrate on the eight key elements:

1. Ethics
2. Integrity
3. Trust
4. Training
5. Teamwork
6. Leadership
7. Recognition
8. Communication

14. Explain Re-Engineering?

Reengineering means systematic starting over and reinventing the way a firm, or a business process, gets its work done, that is, fundamental rethinking and radical redesign of business process to achieve dramatic improvements in critical measures of performance such as cost, service, and speed.

15. Explain Reverse Engineering?

Reverse engineering is the process of discovering the technological principles of a device, object, or system through analysis of its structure, function, and operation.[1] It often involves disassembling something (a mechanical device, electronic component, computer program, or biological, chemical, or organic matter) and analysing its components and workings in detail—for either purposes of maintenance or to support creation of a new device or program that does the same thing, without using or simply duplicating (without understanding) the original.

Reverse engineering has its origins in the analysis of hardware for commercial or military advantage. The purpose is to deduce design decisions from end products with little or no additional knowledge about the procedures involved in the original production. The same techniques are subsequently being researched for application to legacy software systems, not for industrial or defence ends, but rather to replace incorrect, incomplete, or otherwise unavailable documentation

16. What are all the successful attributes of a business analyst?

Business analyst should be a good listener and have empathy towards his or her customer. Business analyst should be highly analytical and result oriented with excellent report writing and communication skills.

17. What is Cross functional team?

For any project that flows through several departments and affects different departments need expertise from all those functions. In such scenarios, companies form cross functional teams. A cross functional team consists of employees from all the concern departments with diversified skill sets, expertise and knowledge.

18. Who are Stakeholders?

Stakeholders are the people who are either affected by the business analysis project or who can affect the business analysis project. It is paramount to involve all the stakeholders to successfully deliver a solution to a business analysis problem. For example in a road construction project the stakeholders are

a. Government
b. Government officials
c. Citizens
d. Contractor
e. Employees of the contractors
f. People who are using the road
g. The shoppers on both the sides of the road etc.

19. What is Process Mapping?

A process is a set of sequential activities carried out in a predetermined order to deliver value to customers. Understanding the existing processes and capturing it in a graphical or IT enabled tool is known as process mapping. Process mapping helps the business analyst and the stakeholder to understand the process and also helps them to identify the issues in the existing process. Microsoft Visio is the most popular software in process mapping.

20. Explain current state, future state and gaps?

These are all the terms associated with process mapping. Current state map refers to capturing the current process in a graphical form. Future state refers to the proposed state of the process. The difference between the current state and the future state processes is known as the gap. If one fills the gap or addresses this gap then automatically the current state process will be moved to the future state. Thus giving the organization an enhanced process compared to the old process.

21. Acceptance and Evaluation criteria – Explain

There is a fine line of difference between the acceptance criteria and the evaluation criteria. Acceptance criteria are the one that must be met to call a solution as a suitable one. Normally acceptance criteria is the acid test to consider a solution whether it is acceptable for implementation. On the other hand, evaluation criteria are the one used when we have several suitable solutions available. In that case all these solutions are evaluated and the most beneficial one is considered for implementation. The following should be considered while designing the criteria for acceptance and evaluation.

a. **Testability**: Anyone testing the criteria should yield the same result. In other words, the criteria should be as objective as possible.

b. **Determine** Ranking and scoring methods for the various criteria.

22. What is Benchmarking?

Benchmarking is the process of comparing one organizational metrics with another organization. It is normally preferred to do this comparison within the same industry but in some cases when such cases are not available we do carryout benchmarking comparison with an organization which is in completely different industry. For example, comparing HDFC Bank with ICICI is benchmarking within the same industry. On the other hand benchmarking HDFC with Apollo Hospitals is across the industry. Benchmarking is one of the most popular tools in Process Implementation. While dealing with Benchmarking we are talking about certain metrics that has been already achieved and demonstrated by someone in our own industry or some other industry. Hence benchmarking gives a strong motivation for the management to emulate some other's performance in their organization.

23. What is Brainstorming?

Brainstorming is a tool to generate creative thinking or out of the box ideas or new thinking in a diverse audience. Brainstorming technique is one of the oldest tools of Business Analysis. In atypical brainstorming exercise about 5 to 7 participants will gather in a room and they have set agenda to generate new ideas on a given topic. There are certain rules to be followed while carrying out a brainstorming exercise. All ideas are welcomed. No one should criticize ideas from participants. It is always encouraged to build upon one's idea by others. Normally the brainstorming exercise can last from 45 minutes to 2 hours. During the meeting, the business analyst should act as a facilitator and should bring in participation from all participants. There should not be any decision making or qualification of ideas during the brainstorming session but should be carried out only at the end of the brainstorming session. It is always better to have participants from diverse areas who have knowledge about the problem area.

24. Business Rules Analysis – Explain

Business Rules are decision making tools that help to run the company and streamline the operation. Business Rules are nothing but the decision path one should take for a given situation. In every organisation each individual will have a set of business rules that helps them to function in a consistent way in their day-to-day operation. For example, for a payment by credit card a company may have the following business rules. Only on everything is satisfied the credit card payment will be accepted by the company.

   i.   The credit card should be in the name of the customer.
   ii. The credit card should be valid.
   iii. The credit card should have the signature of the customer at the back.
   iv. The customer should present another form of government issued ID.

In this above example, whoever works in that company in the capacity of payment collection must adhere to the above business rules. This ensures that everyone works in a consistent manner.

25. What is Document Analysis?

Document Analysis is the technique that any Business Analyst should undertake before commencing any Business Analysis project. Document Analysis is a technique that helps the Business Analyst to understand what all are the different artifacts available within the company that will help him or her to understand the area undergoing business analysis.

Business Analysis is nothing but going through all the relevant document analysis and reports available that are related to the area of business analysis study. One may ask the question where these artifacts are available in a company. These artifacts are known as Organizational Process Assets and companies have two approaches in storing them.

In some companies all these documents and reports will be stored in a library kind of arrangement where it can be easily searched and retrieved. In other companies where they rely on IT, convert these documents into electronic form and store them under Enterprise Content Management (ECM).

26. What is Estimation?

Estimation is the process of arriving at a Ballpark figure (a rough idea) for a given project in terms of cost, time, quality and manpower. There are various types of estimates used by the business analyst:

- Analogous Estimation
- Parametric Estimation

Analogous Estimation:

In analogous estimation a similar project of this size and nature are taken and the same thing is considered as estimate for the given project. For example, you want to construct a house for 1500 sq.ft, you just give a call to your friend who already built a similar size of house and you are finding out from him what is the cost and time it took for building his house.

Parametric Estimation:

In parametric estimation, you break the bigger project into modules and components and then trying to come out with the resources required to carry out those modules and components. For example, you want to get an accurate estimate of your house construction. What are all the things required for the house? They are bricks, cement, sand, iron and steel, wood and fittings. Just writing these and estimating the quantities required under each of these components then multiplying by the respective cost will give an accurate estimation of your house construction.

27. Focus Groups – Explain

Focus Group is a technique that helps the Business Analyst to validate a solution with the help of Subject Matter Experts (SME). In a typical focus group, 20 to 40 participants of SMEs would be invited. They all sit in a room and the business analyst will be acting as a facilitator. The Business Analyst will be presenting a particular solution what he thought of for a given problem. He will be explaining the solution in detail to the SMEs and clarifies their questions. Once he completes his presentation he will ask for the feedback from the focus group. Now it is an opportunity for an SME to evaluate the solution presented by the Business Analyst threadbare. They will give their views both for and against the solution. These SMEs or the members of this focus group helps the business analyst to understand and validate the recommended solution. In a typical focus group session first 30 minutes will be used by the business analyst to explain the solution and the next one and a half hours will be dedicated to the SME responses.

28. Interviews – Explain

Interview is one of the most widely used techniques in Business Analysis Elicitation. Interview is the process of establishing a dialogue with the stakeholder in gathering the requirements. Interview is one of the most efficient forms of requirements gathering because it provides an opportunity to both the interviewer and interviewee to communicate on real time basis. Interview is dialogue rather than a monologue. There are two types of interview, one is telephonic the other is in person. In person is the most preferred one compared to the telephonic. But at the same time it costs more compared to the former. Interview is the efficient tool only when the stakeholders are smaller in size and they are in close proximity meaning in the same region. In case of more number of stakeholders such as 100 or 200 or even more one should be mindful of using this interview technique. In such a case, the business analyst should deploy the interview technique only to a handful of stakeholders such as 20 and for the rest the business analyst should use some other requirements gathering technique.

29. Lessons Learned Process – Explain

In any business analysis project we come across so many obstacles and then overcome them by figuring out a right solution. These obstacles and their respective solution should be recorded in a proper format and stored for future consumption. These records are called Lessons Learned process.

The purpose of lessons learned is to guide the business analyst to gain insights from past mistakes and problems. In a similar problem which happened in the past a business analyst need not have to spend much time in finding the solution rather he can go through the lessons learned process and implement the solution right away. This not only saves the time but also helps the business analysts to avoid trial and error in solving business analysis bottlenecks.

It is mandatory for all the business analysts to do the two following things:

1. Before starting a business analysis project the business analyst should go through the lessons learned process to make himself aware of the various lessons learned in the past.
2. Whenever a business analyst encounters an obstacle or problem in his project and subsequently solves the problem, he should immediately record the problem and solution in the lessons learned process.

30. What is Prototyping?

Prototyping is the process of building a simulated model of the proposed solution in either as a graphical representation on a piece of paper or mimicking the functionality using a computer program. One should not misunderstand prototype as a working model rather it is a model that behaves exactly how the system should function by managing all the parameters. Prototyping helps various stakeholders in understanding and articulating the behaviours of a solution and come out with suggestions on improving it.

31. What is Risk Analysis?

Risk analysis identifies and manages areas of uncertainty that can impact an initiative, solution, or organization. A risk describes an uncertain event or occurrence that may have an effect on the ability of the business analyst, project team, or organization to achieve an objective. Risks by their nature can be positive or negative. Risk analysis involves understanding the risk tolerance levels of the organization, assessing risks, and identifying responses.

32. What is Root Cause Analysis?

The purpose of root cause analysis is to determine the underlying source of a problem. Root cause analysis is a structured examination of the aspects of a situation to establish the root causes and resulting effects of a problem. A critical element of root cause analysis is to ensure that the current business thinking and processes are challenged. That is, do they still make sense or provide good business value in light of current realities?

Fishbone Diagram: A fishbone diagram (also known as an Ishikawa or cause-and-effect diagram) is used to identify and organize the possible causes of a problem. This tool helps to focus on the cause of a problem versus the solution and organizes ideas for further analysis. The diagram serves as a map depicting possible cause-and-effect relationships.

Five Whys: The five whys is a question-asking process to explore the nature and cause of a problem. The five whys approach repeatedly asks questions in an attempt to get to the root cause of the problem. This is one of the simplest facilitation tools to use when problems have a human interaction component.

To use this technique,

- Write the problem on a flip chart of white board
- Ask: "Why do you think this problem occurs?" and capture the idea below the problem
- Ask: "Why?" again and capture that idea below the first idea.

33. State Diagrams – Explain

A state diagram shows how the behavior of a concept, entity or object changes in response to events. A state diagram specifies a sequence of states that an object goes through during its lifetime, and defines which events cause a transition between those states. The allowable behavior of the object is dependent on its current state. There are many titles for the state diagram including State Machine Diagram, State Transition Diagram, and Entity Life Cycle Diagram.

34. What is Structured Walkthrough?

Structured Walkthroughs are performed to communicate, verify and validate requirements. A structured walkthrough is a working session where invited participants review and discuss a set of requirements. Participants are required to ask questions, and make comments and suggestions. Other issues may also be identified during the session. All questions, comments, concerns, and suggestions are recorded. A walkthrough may result in revised requirements as well as issues that require investigation. A walkthrough may also be referred to as a requirements review. An inspection is similar, but follows a more formal process and uses checklists and other tools.

35. Survey/Questionnaire – Explain

Survey is one of the cost effective technique that is available with the Business Analyst. Survey contains a defined number of questions and the respondent will be asked to answer them. There are two types of survey questions, one is open ended the other is close ended. In case of open ended questions the respondents will be asked to answer a particular question based on their idea. These are also called opinionated questions.

For example, what is your view on this particular question is an open ended question? Closed ended questions are generally of true or false in nature or multiple choice questions or rating type questions. The following questions are close ended questions:

i.   Which one of the following is a bird?
   a) Tiger
   b) Lion
   c) Deer
   d) Parrot

ii.   Are you an honest person?
   a) Yes
   b) No

iii.   How do you rate our customer service in a scale of 1 to 5, 1 is low and 5 is high?
   - 1
   - 2
   - 3
   - 4
   - 5

The advantage of survey is you ask the same questions to everyone and this can be conducted at the same time over hundreds of respondents. Thus it saves a lot of money and time for the business Analysis Team. But the downside is because you are not directly interacting with the users. The rate of response will be very low. Typically in a survey only about 20-30% responds to the survey.

36. What is SWOT Analysis?

A SWOT analysis is a valuable tool to quickly analyse various aspects of the current state of the business process undergoing change. SWOT is an acronym for Strengths, Weaknesses, Opportunities, and Threats. SWOT analysis is a framework for strategic planning, opportunity analysis, competitive analysis, business and product development.

Strengths: Anything that the assessed group does well. It may include experienced personnel, effective processes, IT systems, customer relationships, or any other internal factor that leads to success.

Weaknesses: Those things that the assessed group does poorly or not at all. Weaknesses are also internal.

Opportunities: External factors that the assessed group may be able to take advantage of. It may include new markets, new technology, and changes in the competitive marketplace or other forces. Opportunities exist beyond the scope of control of the assessed group; the choices are whether or not take advantage of one when it is identified.

Threats: External factors that can negatively affect the assessed group. They may include factors such as the entrance into the market of a new competitor, economic downturns, or other forces. Threats are also outside of the group's control.

37. User Stories – Explain

User stories are the one that stakeholders use in explaining the functional requirements of a proposed solution. Normally stakeholders are not well versed with business analysis techniques. So they may not be in a position to explain what they want. In such cases business analyst can use user stories as the starting point.

In user stories the business analyst will ask the users or stakeholders to narrate how the proposed system will be used by them and what do they expect out of this proposed solution. They give this explanation like a story narration. This helps the business analyst to get the key functional requirements in the form of a story.

38. What is Vendor Assessment?

Vendor Assessment is the process of evaluating a given vendor whether he will be able to meet the organizational requirements in a given project. The vendor assessment includes:

- Knowledge and Expertise
- Licencing and Pricing Models
- Product Reputation and Market Position
- Terms and Conditions
- Vendor Experience and Reputation
- Vendor Stability

39. Differentiate between Business Analysis and Project Management

Business Analysis is the process of recommending a solution to the management to reach the organizations goals and objectives. Business analysis is nothing but finding one's way in an unchartered sea.

Business Analysis is a non-linear approach which involves lot of research, brainstorming and trial errors to reach the prospective solution. Business Analysis work is building an idea to solve a need, problem or opportunities in this air or on a piece of paper. There is nothing physical about this solution – meaning business analyst does not create any physical or working model.

On the other hand project management is the process of implementing the ideas that were conceptualized by the business analyst in his report. Project management does not work towards identifying a solution but rather meticulously implements the given solution.

40. Differentiate between Business Analysis and Business Analytics

Business Analysis is recommending a solution to the organization. It is a bigger picture working at macro levels to create a huge impact in an organization. It means business analysis aims to create new systems and processes in an organization. On the other hand business analytics is about data mining and getting intelligence out of the data which will support some of the business analysis decisions. In other words business analytics supports business analysis in fact based decision making.

41. What is Business Intelligence?

Business intelligence (BI) is a set of theories, methodologies, architectures, and technologies that transform raw data into meaningful and useful information for business purposes.

Business Intelligence can handle enormous amounts of unstructured data to help identify, develop and otherwise create new opportunities and even it can make interpreting voluminous data friendly. Making use of new opportunities and implementing an effective strategy can provide a competitive market advantage and long-term stability.

Business intelligence allows a company to gather, store, access and analyse corporate data to aid in decision-making. Generally these systems will illustrate business intelligence in the areas of customer profiling, customer support, market research, market segmentation, product profitability, statistical analysis, and inventory and distribution analysis to name a few.

The main objective of Business Intelligence includes:
- ➤ Understanding of a firm's internal and external strengths and weaknesses,
- ➤ Understanding of the relationship between different data for better decision making
- ➤ Detection of opportunities for innovation, and
- ➤ Cost reduction and optimal deployment of resources.

Business Intelligence is used for multiple business purposes, including:
- ➤ Measurement of performance and benchmarking progress toward business goals
- ➤ Quantitative analysis through predictive analytics, predictive modelling, business process modelling and statistical analysis
- ➤ Reporting of departmental/divisional and enterprise perspectives of data visualization, EISs and OLAP
- ➤ Collaborative programs that allow internal and external business entities to collaborate through electronic data interchange (EDI) and data sharing
- ➤ Use of knowledge management programs to identify and create insights and experiences for learning management and regulatory compliance

The methodologies and procedures for implementing such interactive information gathering techniques include:
- ➤ Identifying interview teams
- ➤ Researching organizations
- ➤ Selecting and preparing interviewees
- ➤ Developing interview questions
- ➤ Scheduling and sequencing interviews

42. The career of a Business Analyst

The entry level position of a Business Analyst is at Junior or Associate Business Analyst/Junior Business Analyst. Gradually they move on to become a Business Analyst, then Senior Business Analyst, then Manager Business Analysis, then Director Business Analysis and VP Business Analysis and some may even become CEO. This career path sounds like a dream plan anyone can achieve but there is a difference. Only those business analysts who are meticulously cultivating their business analysis skills and domain expertise can get a guaranteed path like this.

During the last 30 years, we have found so many people who started as an innocent business analyst or heading large global companies today. Why this is possible easily while starting as a Business Analyst? By nature of this profession from the beginning we interact freely and unrestricted with everyone inside the company. We deal with people from bottom most rung to the top most. This gives us a good understanding of the company's business model from day one. What is the role of a CEO? The CEO has a complete grasp of how each department and roles are performing to deliver products of services to the market. Now tell me, how this CEO's position is different from a Junior Business Analyst. Now you may be able to understand that Business Analysis career is a CEO under training.

43. Who is a Subject Matter Expert?

Subject Matter Experts (SMEs) are those who have demonstrated certain degree of knowledge in the given area. Here demonstrated means SMEs are ready reference in case of any issues or clarifications needed in a particular area. Typically SMEs will have more than 10 years' experience with sound academic qualification and required certifications. SMEs are key stakeholders in any business analysis project. First they are the future users of the system. Second, they provide the expert level knowledge required while carrying out the business analysis project.

44. What is a Service Oriented Architecture?

Service-oriented architecture (SOA) is an evolution of distributed computing based on the request/reply design paradigm for synchronous and asynchronous applications. An application's business logic or individual functions are modularized and presented as services for consumer/client applications. What's key to these services is their loosely coupled nature; i.e., the service interface is independent of the implementation. Application developers or system integrators can build applications by composing one or more services without knowing the services' underlying implementations. For example, a service can be implemented either in .Net or J2EE, and the application consuming the service can be on a different platform or language.

Service-oriented architectures have the following key characteristics:

* SOA services have self-describing interfaces in platform-independent XML documents. Web Services Description Language (WSDL) is the standard used to describe the services.

- SOA services communicate with messages formally defined via XML Schema (also called XSD). Communication among consumers and providers or services typically happens in heterogeneous environments, with little or no knowledge about the provider. Messages between services can be viewed as key business documents processed in an enterprise.
- SOA services are maintained in the enterprise by a registry that acts as a directory listing. Applications can look up the services in the registry and invoke the service. Universal Description, Definition, and Integration (UDDI) is the standard used for service registry.
- Each SOA service has a quality of service (QoS) associated with it. Some of the key QoS elements are security requirements, such as authentication and authorization, reliable messaging, and policies regarding who can invoke services.

Why SOA?

The reality in IT enterprises is that infrastructure is heterogeneous across operating systems, applications, system software, and application infrastructure. Some existing applications are used to run current business processes, so starting from scratch to build new infrastructure isn't an option. Enterprises should quickly respond to business changes with agility; leverage existing investments in applications and application infrastructure to address newer business requirements; support new channels of interactions with customers, partners, and suppliers; and feature an architecture that supports organic business. SOA with its loosely coupled nature allows enterprises to plug in new services or upgrade existing services in a granular fashion to address the new business requirements, provides the option to make the services consumable across different channels, and exposes the existing enterprise and legacy applications as services, thereby safeguarding existing IT infrastructure investments.

45. Differentiate between Plan-driven and Change-driven approach

In business analysis process driven and change driven are the two approaches that guide the business analyst in planning the business analysis project. In plan driven approach everything is meticulously thought out before carrying out the business analysis project. Plan driven means there is a complete control over how each step of business analysis project will be undertaken. Plan driven approach is normally adopted in case of high sensitive, high risk and high investment projects.

On the other hand change driven approach is based on minimal planning in performing business analysis project. Most of the decisions are taken as and when required, change driven approaches preferred in case of less investment and low risk projects.

46. What is RACI Matrix?

RACI stands for Responsible, Accountable, Consulted and Informed. RACI matrix helps us to define the roles and responsibilities of various stakeholders involved in a business analysis project.

47. What is a Stakeholder Matrix?

Stakeholder maps are visual diagrams that depict the relationship of stakeholders to the solution and one another. There are many forms of stakeholders map, but two common ones include:

1. A matrix mapping the level of stakeholder influence against the level of stakeholder interest.
2. An onion diagram indicating how involved the stakeholder is with the solution (which stakeholders will directly interact with the solution or participate in a business process, which are part of the larger organization, and which are outside the organization)

48. Differentiate between Collocated and Dispersed Stakeholders

Collocated stakeholders are the stakeholders located in the same building or in the same town. On the other hand dispersed stakeholders are located in different parts of a country, region and even continent. While carrying out a business analysis project especially in the elicitation stage one should be aware of the stakeholder distribution. In case of collocated stakeholders it is relatively easy to schedule and conduct interviews. But on the other hand it involves meticulous planning in case of dispersed stakeholders.

49. What is a work breakdown structure (WBS)?

Dividing complex projects to simpler and manageable tasks is the process identified as Work Breakdown Structure (WBS). Usually, the project managers use this method for simplifying the project execution. In WBS, much larger tasks are broken down to manageable chunks of work. These chunks can be easily supervised and estimated. WBS is not restricted to a specific field when it comes to application. This methodology can be used for any type of project management. Following are a few reasons for creating a WBS in a project:

- Accurate and readable project organization.
- Accurate assignment of responsibilities to the project team.
- Indicates the project milestones and control points.
- Helps to estimate the cost, time and risk.

- Illustrate the project scope, so the stakeholders can have a better understanding of the same.

Identifying the main deliverables of a project is the starting point for deriving a work breakdown structure. This important step is usually done by the project managers and the subject matter experts (SMEs) involved in the project. Once this step is completed, the subject matter experts start breaking down the high-level tasks into smaller chunks of work. In the process of breaking down the tasks, one can break them down into different levels of detail. One can detail a high-level task into ten sub-tasks while another can detail the same high-level task into 20 sub-tasks. Therefore, there is no hard and fast rule on how you should breakdown a task in WBS. Rather, the level of breakdown is a matter of the project type and the management style followed for the project.

In general, there are a few "rules" used for determining the smallest task chunk. In "two weeks" rule, nothing is broken down smaller than two weeks' worth of work. This means, the smallest task of the WBS is at least two-week long. 8/80 is another rule used when creating a WBS. This rule implies that no task should be smaller than 8 hours of work and should not be larger than 80 hours of work. One can use many forms to display their WBS. Some use tree structure to illustrate the WBS, while others use lists and tables. Outlining is one of the easiest ways of representing a WBS.

There are many design goals for WBS. Some important goals are as follows:
- Giving visibility to important work efforts.
- Giving visibility to risky work efforts.
- Illustrate the correlation between the activities and deliverables.
- Show clear ownership by task leaders.

In a WBS diagram, the project scope is graphically expressed. Usually the diagram starts with a graphic object or a box at the top, which represents the entire project. Then, there are sub-components under the box. These boxes represent the deliverables of the project. Under each deliverable, there are sub-elements listed. These sub-elements are the activities that should be performed in order to achieve the deliverables. Although most of the WBS diagrams are designed based on the deliveries, some WBS is created based on the project phases. Usually, information technology projects are perfectly fit into WBS model. Therefore, almost all information technology projects make use of WBS. In addition to the general use of WBS, there is specific objective for deriving a WBS as well. WBS is the input for Gantt charts, a tool that is used for project management purpose. Gantt chart is used for tracking the progression of the tasks derived by WBS.

The efficiency of a work breakdown structure can determine the success of a project. The WBS provides the foundation for all project management work, including, planning, cost and effort estimation, resource allocation, and scheduling. Therefore, one should take creating WBS as a critical step in the process of project management.

50. What is Requirements verification?

Requirements verification ensures that requirements specifications and models meet the necessary standard of quality to allow them to be used effectively to guide further work. Verifying requirements ensures that the requirements have been defined correctly that is, that they are of acceptable quality. Requirements that do not meet quality standards are defective and must be revised. Requirements verification constitutes a final check by the business analyst and key stakeholders to determine that the requirements are:

1. Ready for formal review and validation by the customers and users, and
2. Provide all the information needed for further work based on the requirements to be performed.

At a minimum, a high quality requirement exhibits the following characteristics:

a) Cohesive
b) Complete
c) Consistent
d) Correct
e) Feasible
f) Modifiable
g) Unambiguous
h) Testable

51. Differentiate between formal and informal authority

Each and every one in an organization drives authority through two channels. One is formal and the other is informal. The formal authority comes through the position one occupies in an organization. The person who has formal authority manages his subordinate in terms of working conditions, performance review, pay and perks etc.

Informal authority is derived through certain specific qualities of an individual. We have plenty of examples in history about peoples who wielded informal authority over their followers. For example, Gandhi, Martin Luther King etc.

In case of informal authority, these leaders influenced their followers to do what these leaders wanted them to do but all these happened in the absence of any formal authority. And in fact informal authority is the most powerful than the formal authority.

52. What is Organizational Culture?

Organizational Culture can be defined as a group of people working together with a common goal to deliver certain goods and services to the society and earn profit out of this transaction. As this people are working together in a certain environment over a period they develop certain culture which is known as organizational culture.

Organizational culture is influenced by the culture of the region, the nature of work, educational qualification and vision of the management. As a business analyst one should thoroughly understand the organizational culture in which he is working. Only with this understanding he can successfully carry out the business analysis project and recommended solutions.

53. Differentiate between preventive and corrective action

Preventive actions are those that need to be taken into consideration before the incident occurs. Corrective actions are those that need to be taken to medicate the effect of incident once it happened.

As a business analyst we should be aware of the various risk involved in a business analysis project. For all this risks we should have a plan for preventive and corrective actions.

54. What is a Key Performance Indicator?

KPI is the acronym of Key Performance Indicator. KPIs are those that measure the pulse of the business or a department and its performance. For example, Key performance indicators of a human being are his body temperature, blood pressure, blood sugar, oxygen intake and other vital measures. By defining and using the key performance indicators one can constantly monitor the performance of a business and can take corrective actions whenever the performance is deviating from established standards.

55. What is MoSCoW Analysis?

MoSCoW Analysis is the technique to analyse the requirements. The requirements will be classified as,

- Must have requirements
- Should have requirements
- Could have requirements
- Won't have requirements

Analysing a given set of requirements under technique helps us to visualize the importance and impact of those requirements in a given business analysis project.

> **Must have requirements** are those that cannot be sacrificed at any cost. In case if we have to remove any of the must have requirements then you can very well claim that better scrap the project. Because if you remove a must have requirements you are risking by not delivering a key functional requirements.

> **Should have requirements** are those that falls under functional, performance and regulatory requirements. In most cases you may not be able to remove these requirements.

> **Could have requirements** are those that falls under luxury category. These requirements can be part of the project only when you have budgetary and other resources.

> **Won't have requirements** are those that should not appear in business analysis project. These requirements are basically distractors and do not add any value to the business analysis project.

56. What are Solution Components?

Solution Components are the individual modules under a given solution. For each of these modules there may be several alternatives available. By changing the solution component of a module with another alternative will not affect the performance or functioning of the solution. In other words solution components are helping us to design a solution in a modular approach.

For example, we got to a car showroom and they give us the following options for the same car.

- Two engine types are available that is, E1 and E2.
- Two air-conditioning systems are available i.e., AC1 and AC2.
- Three interior types are available i.e., I1, I2 and I3.

Now in this example, let us understand the difference between solution and solution components. The car is the solution. The modules E1, E2, AC1, AC2, I1, I2, and I3 are the solution components. By having these solution components actually the choice to the customer increases. By interchanging these solution components actually the solution does not differ. With any of these solution components we still call the final solution as car.

57. What are Use Cases?

Use cases explain how a proposed solution will be utilised by the users. For example, let us take how we work out the use cases for a pen. The pen may have the following use cases:

- We should be able to write smoothly for a length of 25 kms.
- The user should be able to hold the pen without mush effort so it should weigh just 50 grams and diameter should not exceed 14 mm.
- The pen should have a cap to protect it from drying and also should have a clip to hold it in a pocket etc.

In the above use cases it is only a sample as we may get about 20 use cases for a simple pen design. In other words use cases are helping us to visualize how the proposed solution will be used by the users. Also it helps us to find out any missing solution requirements.

58. Who is an End User?

The stakeholders are the person who will be intensively using the proposed system on a daily basis to deliver his work. End users are important stakeholders who need to be consulted and brought in before making any decision on a solution. As a business analyst we should be constantly in touch with the end users to understand their problem and concerns and only then we should recommend any solution.

59. What is an Opportunity Cost?

Opportunity Cost can be defined as the income one may get through other activities by not doing the current activity. For example, Kumar is working as a software developer earning Rs. 15,000 per month but he has excellent business analysis skills. If he is joining as a business analyst in another firm he could very well earn Rs. 45,000 per month. This explains that he is looking about Rs. 30,000 per month by not pursuing another opportunity. Here the opportunity cost is Rs. 30,000 which is 45,000 − 15,000.

60. What is a Sunk Cost?

Sunk Cost is the one that is already invested in a project. In some cases when it is a bad investment the money gets locked in and you don't have a way out to take the investment out either by selling or by using the asset. This situation is referred as the sunk cost. In such a situation when the investment is already went bad there is no point in spending more and more money on the same investment to make it good.

61. The Trio

We discussed three characters in the above analogy.

1. Ravi
2. Architect and
3. Civil Engineer

- Ravi needs a house
- Architect gives a shape to the house on paper (drawing)
- Civil engineer builds the house.

Ravi and Architect had a creative discussion to understand the underlying needs and the architect gave the shape to the solution in the form of a drawing. Subsequently the civil engineer built the house and created a product.

What are all the roles represented by these three people?

1. Ravi ..... Stakeholder
2. Architect .... Business Analyst
3. Civil Engineer ..... Project Manager

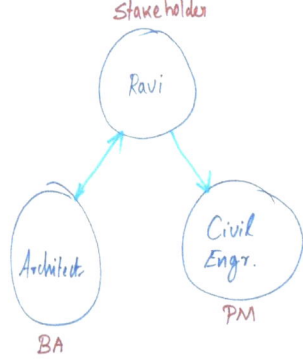

62. Contributions of a Business Analyst

Business Analyst helps the organizations in the following ways:

1. BA helps the stakeholders to visualise the solution without actually building the solution.

   Business analyst does not actually write a piece of code or create machinery. But he defines the solution what need to be created. It may be software, process or machinery. By gathering the requirements the business analyst gives shape to the solution. During the phase of business analysis nothing is concrete in front of us to touch and feel or to see, but the business analyst with his techniques helps the stakeholders to understand how the solution looks like when it is developed and deployed.

2. The above is achieved at a minimal cost.

   The business analyst is helping the stakeholders to visualise the solution at a minimal cost. Since the business analyst does everything on paper, he can change the solution as when required without much impact on the cost. There is nothing physically created so all options are explored in paper itself. Hence the business analyst is giving shape to the solution at a minimal cost.

3. Provides a roadmap to the project manager.

   Project Manager is with an army of resources. They need to be marched in a well identified path just to ensure that the resources are not wasted both in terms of cost and time. The business analysts work gives that roadmap to the project manager so that he marches ahead with his army to realize the product.

63. Who is a Business Analyst?

A business analyst's work can be explained by raising the questions

1. How they do it?
2. What they do?
3. And why they do it?

HOW

- Business analyst is using a set of tasks and techniques to carryout business analysis. This is the BA skill set.
- BA works with a group of stakeholders in a cross functional team. During this the BA understands the need of the stakeholders' vis-à-vis their problems.
- Along with the stakeholders, BA works towards understanding the organization.

WHAT

- Once the problem and the requirements are well understood the BA recommends the solution.

WHY

- The solution developed by the business analyst helps the organization to satisfy a need or solve a problem or to exploit an opportunity. To that extent the goals and objectives of the organization will be met.

64. Complete Business Analyst

As we know in any profession, we need two important groups of skills. One is the professional skills and the other is the set of competencies. For example, take a Medical Doctor. He has the medical skills and also other skills such as communication, investigation skills etc.

Business analyst is like a two-sided coin. On one side he has business analysis skill set (the tasks and techniques). On the other side he has the underlying competencies. The underlying competencies are

- Analytical thinking and problem solving
- Behavioural characteristics
- Business knowledge
- Communication skills
- Interaction skills
- Software applications

Business analyst cannot succeed only with the BA skill set but certainly he needs the underlying competencies as well. The underlying competencies are helping him to carry out the business analysis work effectively. The underlying competencies are explained in separate titles.

65. What is a Need?

Need is a vague statement that describes what the stakeholders want at a very high level. Need is not a defined one. Different people will understand differently.

Let us take an example,
Assume Rahul wants to buy two water heaters for his house. He tells two of his friends about this need and asks each of them to get a water heater for him. Think what will happen. Both will bring two water heaters.

One water heater may be a table top water kettle which can heat a litre of water. The other friend may bring a coal fired boiler. May be Rahul is not satisfied with both the products. This is the result of just processing a need. Because need is a vague and a high level one it cannot guide us to get the right solution.

66. What is a Requirement?

Requirement is a well-defined need in terms of specifications. It describes the need in greater detail so that everyone understands the same way and there is no scope for ambiguities. This is achieved by discussing with Rahul (stakeholders) to understand his need in greater detail.

Rahul's requirements are

- The system shall deliver 100 litres of hot water.
- The system shall deliver the hot water at 70 degree centigrade.
- The system shall prepare the hot water in about 10 minutes from the 26 degree centigrade (room temperature).
- The system shall discharge hot water at the rate of 10 litres per minute.
- The system shall be safe to operate in wet environment.

67. What is a Solution?

The solution is the one that will deliver all the requirements. Solution is the identified software or product that will satisfy all the requirements as intended.

Now Rahul's friends are analysing with some technical experts (system analysts / architects) that what kind water heater will be capable of delivering the requirements. They identified the following solution:

- The system shall be electricity based one as it should heat the water at a faster rate.
- The system shall have 2 meters length of heating filament to heat 100 litres of water in 10 minutes.
- The system shall have a good insulation to prevent leakage of current.

This is called solution design typically documented in "Solution Design Document".

68. Who are Stakeholders?

Stakeholders are the people who have strong interests in the business analysis project. The stakeholders are from two categories of people. One category is the one affecting the business analysis project. And the other category is the one that is affected by the business analysis project.

Take a road construction example. Let us identify the two categories of people.

Category-1: Affecting Road Construction Project

Government & Its Officials

Contractor

Engineers

Citizens

Machinery Leasing Companies

Category-2: Affected By the Road Construction Project

The road users

The shops on both sides of the road

The companies in that area

The local residents

69. Why to involve Stakeholders?

Business analysts closely work with the stakeholders in a cross-functional team. BAs cannot recommend the solution on their own for the following reasons:

BAs are recommending the solution to solve the problems of the stakeholders. So to better understand the problem and to ensure that the stakeholders will be satisfied with a particular solution a BA need to talk to them in detail.

BAs have strong business analysis skill sets and possess a good knowledge of the industry in which they are working. But they cannot be expected to be an expert in everything. So they need to rely on the expertise of stakeholders.

70. How to identify Stakeholders?

Selecting the right stakeholders is very important to the success of business analysis project. Fhyzics uses a proprietary method of selecting stakeholders known as P-S-P approach. PSP stands for Processes, Systems and People.

As soon as a BA gets a business analysis project, he should go through the list of primary, secondary and management processes in his organization. Then select those processes that will be impacted by the business analysis project.

Systems are those applications, software and machineries that sit on these processes to help the process to function better or to automate some activities of the processes. Once the BA knows the process it becomes easy to select the systems as these systems are on the processes.

Who should be the stakeholders in your business analysis project? Yes, it should be the people who have expertise in these processes and systems. So once you know the processes and systems, you can select the people who are connected with them.

71. What is a Process?

Process is a set of activities that are carried out in a predetermined order to accomplish a purpose or to deliver value to the customer. Process helps us to set a standard of performance with in organizations, this result in consistent and reliable processes.

When I make coffee at home, it tastes different each day. But when I walk into a popular coffee chain store irrespective of the location it tastes the same way. Even before I walk into the store, I know how my coffee will taste. At home I don't have any process but the coffee chain has established a process that is followed at all the stores all the time. Hence customer like me gets the same experience day after day.

There are three types of processes:
1. Primary process
2. Secondary process
3. Management process

Primary processes are those that are directly delivering value to the customers. For example, patient treatment process is a primary process of a hospital.

Secondary processes are those that are helping the primary processes to function effectively. IT based billing process is a secondary process of a hospital.

Management processes are those that are governing the primary and secondary processes whether they are performing within the performance parameters. The hospital CEO asks for the attendance report of the employees is a management process.

72. Requirements and its Types

Requirements are the condition or the capabilities required for the organization. The conditions need to be met and capabilities to be acquired by the organization.

Requirements can be classified as Business Requirements, Stakeholder Requirements, Solution Requirements and Transition Requirements. The solution requirements can be further classified as functional and non-functional requirements.

73. Types of Business Analysis Projects

All business analysis projects falls into either of the two buckets. One is New Projects and the other is Process Improvement Projects.

In a start-up organization, the percentage of New Projects is of more percentage. New business analysis projects are launched in organizations to put in place or to create a new system, process, application, software or machineries, which never existed in the organization. In short so far in that organization they never had such systems. It is a common scenario both in start-up organizations and organizations that are in business only for few years typically execute more number of new projects. The new projects are more challenging as they demand more research and involvement from a business analyst and also give excellent opportunity for learning something from scratch and high level of satisfaction.

In mature organizations, the number of Process Improvement Projects will be higher. These organizations are in existence in for several years and the numbers of brand new business analysis projects are relatively rare.

www.ingramcontent.com/pod-product-compliance
Lightning Source LLC
Chambersburg PA
CBHW041117180526
45172CB00001B/296